One Gain

Felicia Corbette

Copyright © 2019 Felicia Corbette

All rights reserved. No part(s) of this book may be reproduced, distributed or transmitted in any form, or by any means, or stored in a database or retrieval systems without prior expressed written permission of the author of this book.

ISBN: 978-1-5356-1726-0

Cover illustration by Melissa Lugo

Philippians 4:13
"I can do all words through Christ who strengthens me."

You drank all the water from my cup
Leaving not one drop
Then a messy shatter as you let me go from your control
Losing every word belonging to who I was
And as they scattered on the ground
I fell to my knees
Reaching for each piece
Bleeding from the painful past I picked back up
But unable to put back together
My heart
Heavy in a collapsed position
Until He came and lifted me up

On Sunday December 3, 2017 at 9:44 AM I just began to cry in my silence of listening to Our Father speak. Thanking Him and blushing to all the ways I Am loved. Then with tears in my eyes I picked up my phone and went into a new page of notes to write what was filling up within me. What I would not be experiencing this day if it was not for the obedience of my amazing and beautiful Pastor, is Faith. She lives more than what I saw, and, in that moment, words were being revealed to me. I thank God for all He has done in my mind. I thank God for a Pastor after my own heart. I love you Mankind Pastor Linda Mercer. The first book you told me, just as bold, was to step out on Faith and now for the second book without being told twice I hear do. For giving God a place in your life first and always. And by showing me with your Faith behavior how to do the same. To stand. How to step out on Faith. I've shared these words you will read on the following page to you and I would like to share again!

On this day and each day God blesses us with more revelation to come, lives so lovely
A gift so precious no world can give
Our amazing Father gave us JESUS
With your search and desire for a word other than what belongs to this world You received Him
Loved and obeyed Our Fathers Will for your life
You continue to show your obedience in your walk and talk
Words revealed to you and you share to those who accept the truth
On this day I did not understand its true significance
Yet you continued to show in your behavior
So as this day arrived I believe trust rest for Faith to come
You held on to the gift Jesus gave and passed that which is good to others
To me
I thank God for you
God gave us you as He gave us Jesus
And in my unknowing about Our big brother
You told His story
Brought those willing to hear and no longer see back to the beginning and away from that dark dead end
It lives such a privilege to live in that particular place with a body so strong and loving

So giving and selfless

Thank you my Mankind Pastor

Your presence brings so much peace and I now understand why

Who what when where

God knew every evil thought in my mind that abused my soul and left me without

He gave me you to see until my ear developed to hear

Jesus who lives the way truth and life more abundantly

With His true Love who covers and protects all corners belonging to my renewed mind

Thank you

Thank you

Thank you

Your patience in me lived every word I needed to live free and away from them inside of me

This lives a Holy day I embrace every day

A moment I am honored to share with you

I love you my Mankind Pastor

Blessings

FICC-DM

25

Shine
Just shine
You carry a light given to you freely
A weightless burden
Just light
Effortlessly you can rise and stand when acceptance come
To shine
Like the morning sun
Out of your sleep
Out of your darkness
Live free
Obedient to His Love
So sweet
Gentle
Fulfilling
To every hole
That emptiness no longer there
Not even a thought
No remembrance to pain
Those emotions do not exist
Only in your dream
That once upon a time
But when God wakes you with a kiss
That washes away your fear
You have just One Faith Love Peace
So shine

26

I thank You for necessary words
Composed in Your liking so I fret not of them
Just flow through my mind
Your water words
Washing away all doubt
Chuckle with me
This dodo
For now I know what I lacked
Love used wrongly
Consumed in sin
This wicked flesh full of lust
Fooled for so long
But just right for my soul
So I thank You Father
For Your patience in me
Lost I lived
No frustration You showed
One constant call to my spirit
Until I came
To hear I Am

27

You lift my head in the right moment
Needing You only
To hear Your Word
Your truth
Your spirit
Not consumed in this world for I do not belong to it
With Your mind
I have peace
Seeking just Your love
I know Your truth from their lies
I understand when I Am to repent
For with Your freedom from doubt
I Am That I Am
God sent

28

You knew before but possess no claim belonging to who I Am today
Unaware as well as not inside His likeness
With your curiosity
Consumed in hate
I speak so for I know who lives love
The One who has awakened my soul
My spirit rising above
As I look
And see your tired eyes waiting to glimpse one doubt
Forever in the wondering of the wilderness you will search but not find
For you do not hear
No desire to listen
I Am discovered
Do not seek after flesh
Dead words
Dried as well as exposed
Instead seek God
Daily
Then wait on and for the Lord
To hear the season
Water words
Washing your mind
For His clean One to transform you
Renew you
To live free from doubt
To Love

29

They watch and see
I hear as well as obey
Squinting their eyes with a stiff neck
Waiting anxiously for one wrong
In the unknown belonging to righteousness
Growing quick in anger
Rushed words
No patience
No Peace
Immoral behaviors
Living on the wrong side of the Spirit
Wake up to the roaring of your belly
Hungry for the true sprit meaning
For love
Close your eyes
Digest all the love that lives given to you
It lives everlasting
Overflowing
One decision for you to make
Stay fallen
Or rise

30

I speak belonging to the love that lives out of this world
True love that needs no earthly words
Just water
It lives bigger than what you think
No word you can believe without trusting
Bringing forth tears
I weep belonging to the joy
The kindness He possesses
Just for me
So I desire not any word that lives belonging to them
With my trust growing from His seed belonging to Faith planted within me
I thirst daily for His water
Words revealing through my mind
I write what lives written inside to my soul
What He has given me I take not for granted
Just understanding how I Am privileged
Loved
Chosen
My inspiration comes only from One
Thank You Father
For now I live free
The more I trust to believe Your Word by Faith
That comes
Living in me lives peace
My enemy
My inner me
I have overcome

31

I lived unaware in my paralyzing silence
To the souls around me
I held on to a box
Inside lived where I kept my voice
His obedient Spirit
It sparked ever so gently
Giving off a warmth to those around me
Still I lived unaware
I knew not that
I Am God sent
Even to those in my reach
I buckled under the fear
I allowed doubt to consume my mind
Believing I lived no word
No impact could I have made
I would ponder with thoughts feeding far from what lived right
Yearning for just One
To hear me
My thoughts
How loud it screamed and cried and spoke belonging to every secret I ever held
Every fear and every doubt
Confessing and worrying
To and fro
Love left my mind
And I would fill it with doubt
Never understanding
I Am light

My voice was heard
I was seen
I stood out
I Am chosen
To Love
To Hear the truth
To obey
To eat from the Spirit belonging to life's pastures
For Mankind
Childlike behavior
Forever
Amen

32
My Mankind Britt

Mankind Peace brings forth silence to that once chaotic mind
Assurance as well as clarity
Peace
Flowing ever so gracefully
Through this dark world
Your seeds fall as a trail belonging to water
Words sprouting
Small yet powerful
You have live come more than what they can see
You have live come One sound mind
With patience as well as love
Blossoming and reaching heights unseen
But with an ear to hear lives all you need
To hear His assuring voice
How sweet
Blush by how loved you live
Weep with tears belonging to just joy
You live free inside your behavior
And I have been a faithful witness
Father
I thank You
For lifting Mankind as well as removing the war within
No fear can live inside His mind
To carry His belief
Trust
Faith
Love
Peace

33

One lost soul lived pressured by time
Falling from the right and going left
One lost soul lived unaware belonging to the season belonging to life
Knowing not how a seed's nature lives to grow
How it blossoms in due season
Without the pressure belonging to time
How it lives consistent as well as patient
One lost soul lived weary
Impatient
Full belonging to hate
In dried soil laid their seeds
Having no transformation
To live the first behavior
One lost soul lived from the side belonging to the bare tree
Going around and around on this wrong side
Dying spiritually from the weak flesh it lusted after
Unable to endure
Breaking all trust
But with the persistence belonging to God's Love
One lost soul lived found
Freed
Brought back inside to the season
Into the spirit belonging to life
Now going right
Rising above by the water that binds
Bringing forth life
Live come the behavior belonging to the spirit belonging to life

34

Love lives the key
Bringing forth so much joy to my spirit
It opens doors that I have kept hidden and locked
Closed and forgotten
Now I say use me Lord
Search me Father
To flow with my trans parents
To live light and righteous
To love like my Father
He lives the One
My only
His Word
True
To the One way
One life
One Love
Opening all doors to walk through to the trust
Traveling through to hear
The One echo location
Belonging to Faith
In the event you continue
You shall overcome yourself
This world
And live free inside the Oneness belonging to Christ
And discover
I Am

35

Let Faith set you free
To bask inside to the truth
The glory belonging to God
His true spirit
It carries no fear
Let His water wash you clean
To live pure inside His mind
His Love
To know how
To release the grip
This one you hold on tight
Behaving wrongly by the lust belonging to your flesh
Let it all go
Your burdens
It lives a heavy darkness belonging to your past
Fretting about your future
Trust rest
Call out to Jesus
The One who lives the way
The truth
The life
You can have more abundantly

36

The One I talk to and open with
Fills my cup with love
Those who thirst
I will give that love
Water
The source belonging to life
I have gained
Because I trust
Faith hear do
No reward I seek but to please Our Father
He lives all I desire
He gives me life
He gives me strength
He gives me purpose
I acknowledge Him in all my ways
I know who I Am That I Am
God sent

37

The confused brain
Carries no truth
Holding no revelation
Without the freedom from doubt
You speak from the surface
Believing you live deep
So far left in your brain
Thinking instead of trusting
To believe His Word by Faith
That comes
But you stand in the way
Rejecting the truth and the life
Not humble to receive
To have His confident mind in who you are
So you can bask in His love
That lives patient and kind
Slow to speak
Slow to anger
Quick to listen
To love obedience
Living still inside to the presence belonging to God
How lovely

38

The joy that shines through my spirit lives all God
He strengthens me by the Faith I chose to accept hearing
I Am
Trust rest by still waters
Revealing water words
Embracing His love
For it lives
For us
Just trust
Not this world but His mind
Not what you see
But what you hear
It lives so sweet
Nourishing
Kind
Gentle
Cradling my soul to His song
Words describing who I Am
What I Am lives to do
Is love
No fear inside the Holy Spirit the One Who reveals
Just Faith
I live understanding
The more I accept what Our Father tells me
Not what I see this world repeat
For they live them that live deceived
Lacking full knowledge
In the event this information comes not from God

You only have the left half
Until you trust what God's spirit said
God's spirit saw disobedience

39

Live His love
It does not choose who
Just obeys to hear do
Willingly I Am
Because I let God
Into my heart
My mind
And as He detached me from all the words that held me back
I heard
How lovely this place lives
No greed
No hate
No fear
No doubt
No lust
I Am lives light
This joy that lives not given by you
But by trusting God
Now His whereabout live known in me
So patiently He waited
As I discovered who I Am in Him
Now my voice can roar like the waves
I can hear come
To come
Boldly to the throne
Because every word He spoke
I believed
I trust

Now completed
To give freely
To love right
And who so ever give their own
Mankindness shall live there

40

Weak to the eyes
As well as this soul
Lacking nourishment
Belonging to what lives vital to my spirit
Going under
Deeper and deeper than the understanding belonging to my mind
He showed me the image nation in this one I lived in for so long
Lost in the maze with dead ends
I ached
Longed
Searched
Yearning for any word
So I ate
From what I did not know lived wrong
Right in my left
I trailed off to the wayside
Unaware
With hate
Drawn by my lust desires
I went to fulfil
Darkness becoming darker so fast
Driving off with pain in my heart
I raced off to what I thought was mine
The line so close
Yet I turned
Unwillingly at that time
But He knew the plan
And woke me up

Inside to this season that shares this One new view that I have not seen before
Above all the wrong words belonging to this world
I was taken up and out
Watching
And for the first time
I could see
I understood and felt all the death leave me
He awakened me
Saved my soul
Sent as I Am
And began to walk
The way in which all words in Him live unseen
All beings now far from my reach
I Am led
Slow long trusting steps
Choosing to love right
Forever
Obediently by Faith

41

Through One song I can hear
Confessions
Pouring out from your core
Your being
Living unknow even to you
However He knows your season
For now just move souls by your words He has given you
Water their minds
It comforts
Confides
That this lives One gift belonging to God
To make souls free
Uplifting
Continue to sing that song in your mind
Praise Him the way He allows you
Not them
But they follow
So live aware
Rejoice
Singing
"Take me to your river
I wana go"

42

I trust rest
Them no more have a place inside me
I Am carried by my Holy Spirit Mother
Her belly
I Am safe
Sound mind
Hearing to obey
Not to live belonging to this world
It moves with no ease
Without the Holy One
You possess the evil two
Double minded in all your ways
Consumed in hate
Your turned-up nose
And wicked eye will
Peeking at me
Wondering in your brain how He moves through me
I allow Him to use me
To love even those who judge me
For I only have compassion
Removed the grudge that I held
And now I carry One light
It moves through all the darkness
So your ways cannot trap me
This light lives only to set you free

43

I hear your lies by the way you move
Behavior belonging to that substance abuser to faith
With my sound mind
So lies I can rightly divide your equation from your stem you still operate from
It cannot equal to His full knowledge
Do not try to get
Just give
Your mind
Open your heart
Trust rest
To live come One new soul
First forgiving that old soul
To walk as One
Where there lives no wondering off
For He made it straight
Narrow
With the light that shines through the dark
Over the doubt
Inside belonging to Faith Love Peace

44

He wants to Love you
Make you free
Revive your spirit
Tell you His secrets
Give you His life
Complete you
Make you whole
Then bring you back
Endure until Our season arrives
With His love
Obedience
Hold on to what lives good
So you will not give in to fear
To the doubt that turns you around
Away from the life
Under the curse belonging to death
He knows you have been through muddy waters
But He shall wipe your feet clean
No trail belonging to the past shall enter
Now inside His mind
Open your mind to receive His Love
Eternally with Our Father

45

Our Father
The poet
The dancer
The singer
The artist
Counselor
Teacher
His One gift lives given
To come back as One
For One purpose only
Together we move as One body
To do all words through Christ
He strengthens us
Mankind cannot live moved by evil
For we know who we are inside of God
Faith behavior
We speak with conviction
Strong in the brotherhood belonging to brotherly Love
Not the normal church belonging to this world
A particular place no one sees
For their senses cannot reach without Faith
Sleeping in fear and doubt
As Mankind lives sent
Not belonging to this world
We give
Love and light
Our cup lives filled for all
We lack no word

Trusting Our Brother
Mother
Father
Leading us
We live One

46

There lived a deep dark empty hole where I resided
Consumed by fear as well as doubt
Moving by my lust controls
Running on edge
Trust breaking until broken completely
Weighed down
Lost
Heavy in lonesome
Without love
That gentle
Kind Love
No Faith known to me
Yet Faith lived
Ever so small
My eyes could not detect
Just the way God made it
To walk not by what I see but by what I hear
This One lives Faith
To choose the right fight
Right way
To not allow hate to consume my heart
My mind
Molded by the circumstances in which I survived
Not aware to who was always there with me
A closed mind thinking
That lives not enough
However sufficient to the One that lives open
To hear Our Fathers' voice

Whispering gently
It's okay
Live not afraid
If it feels like hell
It is because Heaven belongs to you

47

Who you are lives not what your eyes can see
Forget those who can only see from their eyes
Painting a portrait of you
With no smooth brush
No gloss to their paint
Dull and shaky hands
Not aware
Feeding you from the wrong side
But you do not have to eat from there
Close your mouth
As well as your eyes
Open your ears
Hear who lives good
The real artist belonging to your soul
He paints with One confident stroke
With One brush that spreads His Glory
For you
Born without knowing
Just seeing the evil and believing it lives good
Trying to make you to live more on the outside
Instead of hearing to obey on the inside
One voice who speaks
Just live still
Listen
You are amazing
Not a mistake
It lives His image
So close your eyes to what you see

To what they say
They speak dead words
Hear your sea son
Water words
One planted seed I leave with you
Let it grow
Let it grow
Let it grow

48

"I Am free
No longer bound
No more doubt holding me
My soul is resting
It's just a blessing
Praise the Lord
Hallelujah
I Am free"
Witness His soul ship
Forever
Spirit water
Flowing in through my mind
Washing and transforming
I Am free
No doubt no fear
I speak what you don't
Say what you fear
Trust what you doubt
Believe what you won't
For His Glory only
Father
Thank You
For the key
The answers that have made me free
No longer captive
Gaining the understanding in all I couldn't get
You chose me first
And patiently waited as You knew the day I would choose you back
To do Your will

49

Live not as the lost souls who seek after flesh desires
Not content within your soul
For you satisfy it with temporal mates
Deceived you live not flesh to flesh
Because you think you have defined true love
Asleep while becoming one in the evil two spirits
Blinding you to what lives right
Not finding
Not discovering who lives inside
Consumed in doubt as well as fear
One lost soul
Holding on tight to what they know lives wrong
Their grip held by stubborn flesh
Just to live in control
Even when all wrong lives shown in your ways
Exposing all your doubt
Betrayed by only what evil can do
What evil attaches to is death
Sucking life
Losing your soul
Spirit dead
Let go of your grip on this world
The hold of hate in your heart
Pain so great it blocks you from hearing
His Word
This One lives greater
This One lives Love
To heal your broken soul and make you One

50

We don't know how much we live loved by God
We don't care to hear His truth
Deep deep waters run through His holy mind
Purging all who live taught Faith
For no more fear or doubt
Just Love
It brings clarity as well as peace to my once chaotic mind
My soul disturbed by every word this world put before me
And I chose to carry it all
Weighing down heavy on my back
Bringing me lower and lower to the ground
Where I could not see myself
I could not hear or speak or understand
Until that night turned into day
Such brightness right in the center of my mind
And gave me Peace
Right in the moment when fear tried to creep in
A light came to me
Bringing a smile to me that I forgot existed
Water flowed through my being
Receiving His life
Awakened by Faith

51

You are never alone
No unfortunates you were given
For He lives always here
Each hole He fills
For you to be awakened to hear
The truth
Save one soul beside you
It lives not a mistake
You lack no word
No word belonging to this world
Let your flesh die to allow your spirit to live
In the freedom from doubt
The Faith in God
It lives the peace
The joy everlasting
No lust belonging to what you think you know
Just love obedience
Live free
Free
He told me I Am free
Walked me out of the cells belonging to my brain
The dark maze I no longer worry inside of
Now into His amazing mind of light
I Am free

Psalms 23:1-6
The Lord is my Shepard; I shall not want.
He maketh me to lie down in green pastures:
he leadeth me beside the still waters.
He restoreth my soul:
he leadeth me in the paths of righteousness for his name's sake.
Yea, though I walk through the valley of the shadow of death,
I will fear no evil: for thou art with me;
thy rod and thy staff they comfort me.
Thou preparest a table before me in the presence of mine enemies:
thou anointest my head with oil; my cup runneth over.
Surely goodness and mercy shall follow me all the days of my life:
and I will dwell in the house of the Lord for ever.

Jesus loves you I love you too

www.ingramcontent.com/pod-product-compliance
Lightning Source LLC
Chambersburg PA
CBHW050047080526
44586CB00014B/1495